Stocks

Penny Stocks

Make Money!

Top 10 Simple Secrets for Penny Stocks, Investing and Stock Trading

2nd Edition

A.Welch

© Copyright 2015 by A. Welch - All rights reserved.

Table of Contents

A.Welch

6

Introduction

I want to thank you and congratulate you for downloading the book, *"Stocks: Penny Stocks – Make Money – Top 10 Simple Secrets for Penny Stocks, Investing & Stock Trading"*.

Who does not want to make money? I bet no one. Do you want to have investments that continually bring in money? I bet you would. However, the greatest challenge is how to go about making money. Investing in stocks is a great place to start. However, not everyone has all the funds that the normal stock markets require. So, what next? Do you stop investing just because you may not have as much money to buy a share at over $10 probably? Not all hope is lost as you can still invest in the stock market even with as little as less than a dollar for a share. How, you ask. Penny stocks' trading is the way to go. I am sure you have heard about penny stocks trading probably from the movie "Wolf of Wall Street". However, do you really know what penny stocks are?

This book explains what exactly penny stocks trading are. By reading this book, you will get to know how to invest in penny stocks as well as how to make it big, as investing in penny stocks and making it big are very different. You will also get to learn essential tips and tricks for being successful in penny stocks trading. You will also learn the common mistakes that people make when investing in penny stocks and how to avoid them if you want to be successful in penny stocks trading. This book also contains valuable knowledge on day trading penny stocks, common terms used in penny stocks and basically all you need to be successful in penny stocks trading.

Thanks again for choosing this book, I hope you enjoy it!

Penny Stocks: What Are They

If you are familiar with the movie "Wolf of Wall Street" or Jordan Belfort's story, then you most likely to know what Penny stocks are. Simply put, penny stocks is a common word in the U.S. used to refer to typically low priced stocks that can range between $5 and $10. These stocks may also be referred to microcaps. Penny stocks trade between $0.0001 and $4 per share with these stocks showing extreme price fluctuations of 25% to over 100 within short trading periods. What this means is that you can maximize in great price increases and sell your stocks making lots of money in the process.

Penny stocks, contrary to the name, are hardly ever just worth or priced at a penny. These stocks are also known by another name in other countries outside the United States: cent stocks. Penny stocks are, legally speaking in the United States, securities whose market prices are less than $5 per share, not listed or traded in any national exchanges like the New York Stock Exchange (NYSE) and not able to meet other important criteria set by the Securities and Exchange Commission or the SEC. In Europe, particularly the United Kingdom, penny stocks are securities that trade below £1 per share. In the United States, penny stocks are normally transacted over-the-counter, i.e., outside formal or centralized stock exchanges, like the Over-The-Counter (OTC) Bulletin Board or via Pink Sheets. The Financial Regulatory Authority (FINRA) in the United States operates the OTC Bulleting Board for members who subscribe to said medium. Unlike exchanges like the NYSE or Nasdaq, the OTC Bulletin Board isn't electronic. In the United States, penny stocks trading is covered and regulated by rules and regulations defined by the FINRA.

Companies that issue penny stocks normally have low market capitalization due to the low market or trading prices of their shares. As such, penny stocks can be quite unpredictable or volatile, which makes some people to be a little conservative when it comes to investing in them as they are usually tied to the success or failure of a business prospect. Firms commonly float these stocks with little or no real assets such as prospecting firms that deal in oil, mining and such like activities. These types of firms usually have short, fluctuating or no consistent record of accomplishment of earnings, which makes trading in penny stocks – however lucrative – high risk.

Further, volatility can at times be due to manipulation by investors with access to funds that are even bigger than the stocks' total market capitalization. Investors who fall victim to manipulated penny stocks are often into get-rich-quick schemes. The actual face value of a penny stock will be manipulated and turned big. So in essence, the price of the stock is not an indication of the company's true worth. So if you give into this kind of a stock, then you must remain prepared for any consequence that the stock might throw up. Given such risks, you'll need to tread carefully if you're considering getting into or are already trading in penny stocks in order for you to take calculated risks that will enable you to significantly increase your chances of enjoying huge returns and minimizing your risks of losing money.

Most of these low priced companies do not attract many investors because of their zero trading volume; however, the good thing is that you can maximize on this, make sound investments decisions and reap huge returns.

A.Welch

Understand This Before Trading In Penny Stocks

Penny stocks, as you know, are low valued stocks that are traded in the market or over the counter. These stocks will see sharp rises and falls and it is up to the trader to capitalize on this trend. But before you can go ahead and start investing in penny stocks, you need to know some few basic things about penny stocks.

Information

Because penny stocks aren't publicly traded, i.e., not listed on big and organized exchanges, adequately available information on most of them may be quite limited for the investing public, which makes it extremely difficult to get some credible information since companies listed on the pink sheet. It's because companies that issue penny stocks aren't required to file with the Securities Exchange Commission. As information on such companies aren't as abundant as for those whose stocks are listed on big organized exchanges like the NYSE, the relatively higher potential earnings come with higher risks as well. You may think your broker will provide you with enough information about these stocks. But he or she might know just as much as you would. The two of you are in the same boat. In that, he might have a slight upper hand and know a little more about it than you would. So it will not hurt to find out from them about it. Call them up and tell them the name of the stock. If they find the information for you then well and good but if they don't, then don't worry, if you have heard of the stock as a good one then it surely must be good!

Liquidity Risk

What is liquidity? In the context of investing in penny stocks, it's the ability to be able to sell – also known as "liquidate" in financial circles – your penny stocks at the exact time or price that you need to. Liquidity risk is the risk or the possibility that you may not be able able to liquidate your penny stock holdings when you need to and at the price you want to.

Penny stocks trading poses this risk especially when supply is greater than the demand. As earlier indicated, not many people are usually very willing to invest in penny stocks because most investors, unlike you, are too risk-averse and would rather settle for average returns just to be able to lower their risks. Low liquidity will mean that there will be a difficulty in finding a buyer for a given stock, as this might mean that you lower your share price to an extent where it might be deemed attractive to other buyers in the market. Low liquidity is normally a loophole for some traders to manipulate the prices of stock. So understand what you are getting into before you decide to buy a stock for yourself. The liquidity of a stock is always a matter of consideration for any trader, small or big. After all, you cannot hold on to a penny stock forever and will have to duly dispose it off at some point in time. So it is important that you pick those that are actually being traded regularly and you are not choosing those that are traded randomly or once in a blue moon. Your diligence is everything when it comes to picking penny stocks.

Common Terms Used In Penny Stock Trading

If you want to invest in penny stocks successfully, you would need to be aware of some few things. These terms are regularly used in the penny stock trade market and if you wish to be part of it then it is important for you to be well versed in them. They will give you a fair idea of some of the ways in which the penny stock market operates and help you understand the basic pattern that you must follow when you wish to get started in this trade.

Day Trading

This is a common term used in penny stocks investment. Day trading refers to the buying and selling of penny stocks with the goal of making a profit from the difference between the buying and the selling price, on the same day. So in effect, the trader aims at buying the stocks when they are priced lowest and then sell them at the highest price during the day. This can be done by choosing the buy and sell triggers. It will be tough at the very beginning to choose the exact numbers but with time, you will know to predict how high a stock will rise. Remember that the stocks will not follow a predictable pattern and you must understand it by studying it carefully. Some stocks might rise during the wee hours of the market and then fall and some might follow the reverse pattern. It is important to note that in the U.S unlike in the U.K, where penny stocks are traded in the stock exchange, penny stocks are traded over the Counter Bulletin Board and pink sheets.

Due Diligence

Before making a decision to buy a stock, it is prudent to practice the rule of due diligence. Due diligence is a common terminology used in trading of penny stocks and is usually abbreviated as DD. In this case, DD is simply, doing some background research before deciding to buy a stock. Remember that you cannot gamble with these stocks, as they can be quite unpredictable. You will not know if the stock is good or not based solely on its price fluctuations. You have to study it carefully and understand whether or not it will give you good returns. Pick up the stock's data and start going through it carefully. Don't assume a stock as being good just because many people have bought it. There is a risk of over buying that will loom over the stock and it is important for you to carefully evaluate the stock's true worth and use your DD to separate the good ones from the bad ones.

Stop Loss Percentage

Another term you will hear often is Stop Loss Percentage. This is simply the maximum percentage at which a trader can take a loss. If you happen to set your stop loss at say 10% and the value of your invested stock happens to fall by 10%, you can willingly relinquish your shares and accept the 10% loss to preserve your capital. This is extremely important for a penny stockholder. Most traders will worry that they will have to settle for a loss when there was a chance to not take an exit on it and wait for it to move forward again. But that is the wrong thought to have. If you wait for it to go forward then you might waste time. Instead, you can either assume position from the same place or move to a better stock. In all, you will not risk your capital getting stuck in a place and have the chance to use your capital to your advantage by implementing the stop loss mechanism. Let us look at an example. Say you bought 100 stocks of company "A" at $0.95; you are hoping it will go up to $1 by the end of the day. But you must place a stop loss of 10% in case it does drop to that price. So set your stop loss at $0.88. This will ensure that you exit at that point and don't have to take it if it goes any lower than that.

Swinging

Swinging refers to exiting at the stop loss mark and then assuming a fresh position from there itself. The basic idea here is to capitalize on the stock's volatility and cover the losses. The general belief is that a stock will steadily rise in value once it hits a low. So as soon as the stock exits at the lowest mark, it will start rising again. Most traders prefer to place another stop loss at this point in time to ensure that they don't undergo a loss. Again, you must choose the 10% cover and set the stop loss. Don't underestimate the true value of the stop loss mechanism and put it to regular practice.

Ask

This is the practical share price acceptable at a particular moment at which you can buy shares. It is the price that you are asking for a share. You are valuing it at that price and think it is the best value for the stock. The ask price will depend on your analysis of the stock. You will know to judge a stock only after studying the market for some time. Many people set such low values and you wonder if they are wrong in setting such a low ask price. But then you will realize that the stock's price has really fallen to that price and that they have truly gained from their assessment. Similarly, you must also study the markets carefully and then decide on the ideal ask price for a share.

Profit Percentage Gain

This is used to refer to the maximum percentage at which a trader has pegged their profits. A trader will always enjoy profits whenever the stock rises by set profit Percentage gain. This is obviously calculated based on the buy and sell price of the share. Every trader will have expectations out of their investments and they will decide on the percentage profit based on what they wish to gain from the difference in prices of the stocks.

Bid

Bid refers to the buying price of shares.

Here is a brief process of how trading in penny stocks is likely to go:

1. Start by practicing due diligence. This will involve doing some research beforehand to come up with a list of stocks you might consider trading for that day.

2. Use your own judgment to gauge on the reaction of the market and then pick one stock.

3. Buy the shares.

4. Sell your shares when the percentage profit gain of your choice has been attained. Go on and on trading in that procedure for trading in penny stocks and make profits. We will look at this process in detail to help you get started on trading in penny stocks.

Volume

The volume, as you know, is the total number of shares that are traded at any given point in time in the share market. This volume keeps fluctuating every second as some ones ask price will match someone's bid price. This type of matching can occur all through the day and at no point will the volume fluctuations remain stable. They will keep fluctuating all through out and you can keep looking at it in your software. Penny stocks will also have volume fluctuations all through the trading hours and at no point will it stabilize unless the stock price freezes owing to excess buyers or excess sellers.

Broker

The broker is your helper who trades the stocks for you. You cannot trade in the stock market without being a member of the stock exchange. The broker will represent the company that is a member of the exchange and help you buy and sell the stocks. He or she will also advice you on a few good stocks and tell you whether or not you should buy a stock. But the final decision rests with you and you will only have to trust your judgement combined with your research on the stock.

Commission

Commission is what the broker will charge you for the services provided. He or she is putting in efforts to help you buy and sell stock and also suggest some. For that, they will charge you a commission. But not all that is deducted will go to the broker alone. Some of it will go to the brokering company as well. The commission varies from company to company and you must pick the one that has on offer the lowest rate. But if you don't wish to compromise with the quality then you can choose one that offers a higher rate but good brokers.

Limit order

Limit order refers to the sell price that you wish to attach to your stock. This sell point is where your stocks will be sold. You have to instruct your broker and tell him clearly that you will not settle for a penny less. This is mainly because you would have calculated a percentage gain and even a short margin could make a big difference in the gain. There are softwares that allow you to set the price yourself so that your stock is sold as soon as it reaches the price. You don't have to keep tracking the price and will be notified as soon as the stock is sold.

Portfolio

Your portfolio is your investment sheet. It will contain all your investments and mention details of all your holding stocks, sold stocks, stock number, stock value, bought price, sell price, realized profit, unrealized profit etc. All of these are important for you to gaze upon in your portfolio statement. You will also see the trend that you have been following in terms of buying and selling your stocks. You must always look at your portfolio at the end of the day to cross verify whether or not your stocks are being traded correctly. If you spot any errors then have it rectified at the earliest.

Stock split

Stock split refers to a company splitting the stock in two to increase the number of stocks available in the market. This is done when there is a lot of absorption and not many people are floating their shares in the market. The company will be interested in pumping back the shares and increasing their market capture. This is a good thing for penny stocks and if you are holding any at the time of announcement then you will receive what are known as bonus shares. These will help you earn a greater profit.

Bullish reversal

A bullish reversal refers to the price of the stock going upwards. This happens if the lowest is lower than the previous day's low and the current price is higher than the previous day's close. So the stock will move upwards and the trend will help you realize a profit if you are holding on to any of the company's stocks. This trend will occur when there are more buyers for the stock and less sellers. You can capitalize on the situation and sell all your stocks to arrive at a profit.

Bearish reversal

The bearish reversal is the opposite of the bullish reversal. It occurs when the current price is lower than the yesterday's close. This pattern is a downward trend. It appears when many people sell their stocks all at once. The trend can cause you a few losses on certain bad stocks.

These are just some of the terms that you must understand and gaze upon when you wish to indulge in penny stock trading.

A.Welch

FAQs About Penny Stocks

When you start trading in penny stocks, it's obvious that you will have a few questions pop into your mind. In this chapter, we will look at some basic questions that get asked on the subject and answer them to help you understand the concept better.

Let us start.

Are penny stocks good for me?

Yes. Penny stocks are a great choice for both beginners and established traders. Penny stocks will help you understand the stock market and how it operates. Once you start trading in penny stocks, you will know exactly how the stocks rise and fall and whether or not you must sell the stocks that you hold. Although it is best to first observe the market as an outsider and then start trading, you can start off with it if you have the confidence to do so. Penny stocks will pay you good money provided you time the market and know exactly how to pick and hold the right stocks. If you have already been investing in the stock market then you will easily slide in and make a smooth transition. You must understand the difference between regular and penny stock trading though and formulate a different strategy to make it big.

Can I do just penny stocks?

Yes. The choice is completely yours. If you think you can make a lot of money through penny stocks then you can do so. But remember that you will have to trade carefully as you are investing your entire capital in just one form of trading. It is a basic rule in the stock market to diversify your risk and not do just one type of thing. It is up to you to diversify your capital or invest all of it in one place. Not that it's a bad thing but you must practice trading carefully and not making mistakes that can cause you to lose money.

Should I sign up somewhere?

No. There is no such rule that you must consult a company that provides penny stock advice. But if you think it is better to consult an expert and understand the penny stock market through their view then you can sign up with a reliable site that provides advice on penny stocks. However, don't sign up with something that looks suspicious and choose a company that promises to give you all the best picks. And once they do give you their picks, it is up to you to choose and stick with it or choose something else depending on your analysis. Different people will view the stock market differently and it is up to you to assess it in the best possible way.

Will I get regular recommendations?

Yes. You will get recommendations from the company you signed up with on a daily basis. But if you are going solo, then a reliable news channel will employ experts who will suggest their picks to you. You can look at the suggestions and choose stocks that you think will do well in the market. Your broker will also suggest good stocks to you, as they will get certain tip from the stock market analysts. But don't blindly take whatever they offer to you and do your own research before taking up a stock. It pays to study the stock for a week or a month and only then decide on it. Remember that these penny stocks are pretty predictable and you can understand the pattern they will follow by observing them for a few days.

Will they give me a stop loss price?

Yes. When somebody gives a suggestion, they will also supplement it with a stop loss suggestion. Stop loss is an important part of any stock market strategy. If you don't make use of one, then you will end up getting stuck with a bad stock for a long time. Instead, it is best to get rid of the stock and not bother about it. Many people think it is best to not use a stop loss and hold on to the stock. But that will turn into a long-term investment, and your money will be locked up for a long time. Instead, it is best to sell the stock and take a temporary loss, which can be easily compensated later.

What's the best trade strategy?

That depends on you and varies from person to person. There is no one strategy that is universal. If you wish to become a contrarian, then so be it. If you wish to be a fundamentalist, then do your homework first. If you wish to invest in stocks using your knowledge on technical then you can do that as well. The choice is completely yours and you can pick whatever you think will work for you. But don't trust someone else's opinion and their strategy, as what works for one might not for another. Even if two people start out with the same capital and the same stocks, one might make wise choices and the other one stupid choice. So it depends on your trading skills and you must pick a strategy that will work for you.

Is there a minimum capital required?

No. The capital to invest depends on how much risk capital you are willing to invest in the stock market. As you know, there is a lot of risk associated with these stocks and you must choose them wisely. It's better to start with a small capital, and then increase it as you go. That will ensure you know what you are getting into and whether or not you should introduce fresh money. Certain stocks will require you to invest a minimum amount, but given the stocks' low prices, you won't have to spend too much in just one company's stocks.

Does it need full time attention?

No. Many working professionals indulge in penny stock trading, as it will pay them well. You don't have to keep staring at the screen to observe any fluctuations in the prices. You can set alerts that will tell you whether or not a stock is moving fast enough and you need to take quick action. You will also have your broker's assistance; who will observe the trend in the stocks, for you, and tell you when it is best to buy them or sell them. But if you are very serious about it, then you must spend time indulging in it and understanding it thoroughly. You can then start trading regularly, and if you think it is worth quitting your job for then you can take that option as well. But remember, taking up penny stock trading full time is a risky thing to do, and you must thoroughly understand all the pros and cons of it before deciding to go professional with it.

Can I trade daily?

Yes. In fact, penny stock traders are considered day traders. They are meant to buy and sell on a daily basis and make several small profits from it. So pick the stocks that are volatile and go down and up within a single day. But you need to be careful and pick the stocks that are slightly predictable. Choose the ones that drop during the initial hours of trading and then rise up by the end of the day. That will ensue you get the stocks at the lowest and sell it at the highest.

Can I hold and earn?

Yes. You can hold the stock and earn from it. Certain penny stocks will gain overnight and you can take advantage of the situation. But you must know what to hold and what to dispose off to benefit from it. Some stocks might also lose points over night, and it is important for you to sell such stocks on the same day as you buy them.

These are some of the most common questions that get asked on the topic and hope you had yours answered.

A.Welch

Getting Started With Penny Stocks Trading

When starting out with penny stocks trading, it will be prudent to start with paper trading. This is the use of fake money to trade, instead of diving in straight with your hard-earned money. Just take some time to learn well about penny stock trading even for a month to get a feel of your skills. Record your results, as this will give you the needed confidence you require before you can start trading. Once you are sure of your skills you can set up an online broker account.

For you to start you need to have some tools to get you started in order to trade well in the penny stock market. The following items are essential to get you started on penny stocks trading especially if you want to start trading online:

A reliable computer

A good computer is essential to get you started. If you want to trade online, you would not want hindrances due to for instance computer failure or inability to the computer to process your orders in real time. Get a good computer that can serve you for quite some time.

It is best to have a dedicated computer table to place your computer on and not use it for anything else. Don't allow others to access it and make sure it is meant only for you to use and work on. This should extend beyond the working hours of the market and you must not store any other data on it. You will have to take it very seriously if you wish to make it big in the stock market. Having a casual attitude about it will not cut it. If you decide to get yourself a laptop then ensure that it is not moved around. Give it a proper place and ensure that you reach there on time every day, before the market opens and do your early morning research. To conduct your research, you will require the following important aspect.

Reliable Internet connection

Since you will be trading online, you need to get fast Internet connection. As earlier indicated prices can vary very quickly meaning that you need to be on the lookout and if there is a sudden change in prices make the most suitable decision. Unreliable Internet may disappoint you especially when you need to make a quick decision. The risk doubles when you conduct day trading. As you know, the prices vary within split seconds. You will wonder how something so low could bolt up within a few seconds or how something so high could drop so soon. If your internet gives you problems then you will end up not making the best use of a price fluctuation and lose out on good money making opportunities. So it is best to get the fastest possible Internet connection and have two separate stations to access it.

Brokering company

The next thing to take up is a brokering firm. Pick a good one for yourself. There are many choices and you can choose the one that offers you the best commission rates. You can ask someone to suggest to you the best company in their opinion. You can also look up online to know the best one. Once you decide, personally go down and fill out the forms. You might have to carry a few personal documents for the registration and can ask them by calling them up in advance.

Special broker

Once you choose the firm and open your account, you must choose the right broker as well. There might be penny stock specialists, who might help you get set up and understand the functioning properly. Ask the firm to suggest the best penny stockbrokers to you and employ the best one. Remember that you must develop a good rapport with your broker if you wish to make it big. There should be no discrepancies and the two of you must be on the same page for it to work out for you.

Trading Software With Real-Time Data

You would also need the best real-time data feed application in order to trade in penny stocks. It is crucial that you trade on real-time data, as you would not want to make a decision on some data that is outdated, as making such a decision can cost you a lot of money.

This software can be downloaded from the Internet. It can also be availed through your app store. But it will be easiest to get if you ask your brokering company to help you have the software installed in your computer. In fact, it is best to choose the software that your broker himself uses so that the two of you can be on the same page. Many types of software also allow you to buy and sell the stocks by yourself. All you have to do is login and set buys and sell calls. This will ensure that you don't waste any time conferring with your broker and buy and sell the stocks at a fast pace. But before you do so, it is important to understand the process thoroughly lest you make a mistake while choosing the buy and sell numbers.

Journal

You must maintain a journal. Although you can easily take notes in a digital diary, it is best to maintain a hard copy of all your notes. Write down any notes that you wish to refer to and also any references that you wish to remember in the future. Remember that these notes will come in handy in the future and are important things to consider, which cannot be taken lightly. Don't lose the journal though and keep referring back every now and then to know the best time to buy and sell the stocks.

Now that you have rough idea of what penny stocks trading is and have all the necessary items with you, what next. The next step is to start trading. As earlier indicated, rather than start trading with actually money, you should instead start with paper trading first. Once you have learnt about penny stocks trading, then you can start trading with real money.

Paper Trading

To practice paper trading, it is good to make sure you have all the requirements to start. Once you have your fast reliable computer and Internet connection, you need to have suitable software to record your paper trading results. You will have to learn to wake up earlier before the market opens so that you can do your research before going into a day's trading. The penny stock market normally opens at 9.30 EST. Using your software go over it and look at any relevant news and filings. Pick out the stocks that have released "WOW" press releases and put them in your watch list for that particular day in case you are using MicrocapFeed. You can also make another watch list for trends to get so that you can track certain trends.

Now prepare a watch list for yourself. This watch list should contain all the stocks that you either wish to trade in or are already holding. It has to be comprehensive and include all the stocks that you are interested in tracking. Once the market opens, you won't have the time to add a stock at a time. You must be prepared in advance and ready with your watch list before the opening bell goes off. But wait for the rates to settle down a little and don't get over excited by the fluctuations in the numbers that happen.

In your watch list, make sure the supply side of the stocks you are watching are getting to minimum and if the opposite is the case, then you need to pull out any such stock from your watch list. Also make sure no S-8 for any stocks you are watching were filed recently to the stock exchange commission as this will be an indication of old news or small news. Also, check earlier Press Releases of that company to make sure there is no news overdose on the stocks you could be watching on your watch list. The simple essence of doing this is to make sure you have filtered well the stocks you will be following up eliminating the less attractive ones.

When the opening bell goes, watch the stocks on your watch list to see if your prediction reflects the actual traffic of demand on them. The volume has to be high and ensure that people are also buying.

Another important thing to note is that the number of people buying is greater than the number of people selling. That should be a good indication of prices going up. The bid should be tight; a large gap is a reason to move away. This is where many people go wrong. Don't assume your stock will keep rising up if there are very little sellers and too many buyers. The ones who think they will not get the stocks owing to less number of buyers will decide to pull out of it. This means that the number of buyers will drastically reduce and the sellers will meet their ideal buyers. There is also the danger of over buying, which will cause the stock's price to plummet.

Decide on how many shares you will buy and at the price, you are willing to buy them. Take your amount of funds you are trading with for that day, in our case it is $1000 dollars and divide it by the asking price; it's that simple. This should give you the number of shares for the day that you want to buy.

Using your earlier set percentage gain limit, wait until your limit has been attained and sell your shares at that profit; don't be greedy. Instead, just take it and count yourself lucky as a little patience might send you on the regretting end. Go ahead and put down your outcomes on your paper-trading portfolio. Repeat the paper trading for a few more days; it can even be for a month to see how well you are doing after which you can now go in full swing with real money.

All said and done, many people will struggle to settle for the price that they wish to sell it at and think it will keep rising and wait on it. But you have to have a strong determination to do the right thing and not think about the price going higher. If it reaches your price then exit immediately. Besides, a few extra points won't give you a sky rocketing amount.

Below is a summarized systematical baby steps to have you get into full action as you now decide to involve your real funds in the penny stocks:

> ➢ First, remember to meet the requirements including the legal requirements. Go through the instructions manual and ensure that you have understood everything there is about penny stock trading.

> ➢ You need to sign up with an online broker and fund that account with cash. It can be E-trade, Scot trade, or even Fidelity.

> ➢ Use the steps used in paper trading and do everything except this time round you will involve real money

> ➢ Set Investment amount

You will need to have a figure of how much money you are ready to put into the investment of penny stock trading. Simply have your figure right. It could be $ 1000 or $700; you will use this amount to buy shares worth your amount of capital. Remember that this is your initial investment and you might need more as you go. So think of splitting this amount and investing $700 for now and holding on to the $300 to pump in once the $700 has been fully invested.

*Get down to simple math

You will need to multiply your initial amount by 3. Why? In order to trade every day, you will have to multiply your initial amount by three and wire it to your online account. For instance if you had set $ 1000 for a single stock, then you will require $ 3000. It all depends on your initial figure that you have set.

How it works

Assuming you bought $1000 worth of shares on Monday, and then you decide to sell it when the stock goes up by say 10% this will imply that you have made $100 profit plus commissions. Profit will be 10 % of $1000 and then add the given commissions say $20. In essence, you would have made $120 on Monday on top of your investment. Now see why you had to multiply your initial amount by three. It is because you will have to repeat the process on Tuesday and Wednesday. Here, the company will not pay you the money immediately. They will obviously have to free your money and return it back to you. That is why you have to understand your limit. So the processing will take some time and you have to continue trading in the meantime. By Thursday, the money you used will be ready for use on Friday. This is because there is usually a three-day settling period when you buy or sell a stock before the cash can be ready for use again. This is very important to eliminate incurring opportunity cost which is the cost foregone when you leave your funds idle.

How to buy penny stocks at lowest price

The Ask is the real-time lowest price someone can be willing to sell the sock for while the Bid price on the other hand is the real time highest price another person is willing to buy a stock for. Once you get to understand those two, you may have to place your bid at 10% or more above the current ASK price. This normally is applicable in highly competitive trades when demand surpasses the supply. Set your entry point with your bid price at an initial of 10% instead of placing a bid on an order that will require more modifications. It is best recommended not to place an order on an (AON) all-or-non-simply because it will allow your broker to fill your order when all the shares at your specified price become available. It is best to have at least some shares instead of none.

Avoid chasing penny stocks that are in excess of 50% when there is a buying rush. This is simply because you will be trying to buy a stock that is suddenly going up. It is best to buy a stock after the first 20 to 30 minutes of the trade opening. From past experience, rapidly growing stocks take a sudden shift back to low before the share price shifts up again.

If you are a serious penny stock trader then you will have to take the above-mentioned advice very seriously. It is vital that you understand how a stock should be bought at its lowest price. Even if you are a beginner, don't jump into it to get hands on experience. The stock market is not a very forgiving place and won't allow you to get away with a lucky streak. You must spend some time understanding all that there is to, about the particular penny stocks that you have chosen to trade with. Then you must observe the market trends and spend some time in front of the computer. Once you have surmised the trend of the stock, you must place a buy bid for it at the correct ask price. And even if it goes down by a little after that, you must not worry but if you do it the right way, then it will not go down at all.

How to sell penny stocks at high prices

It is best to exit your position when the stock price is going up. When the prices go up, normally it is because buyers are thronging in to buy. If you wait for the prices to go down you will get in contact with other shareholders who might want to exit due to current decreasing share price. This means the best sell you might make is the bid price, which is not the price for a seller. The trick is buying early and selling early.

But this early is not too early. You must wait until such time as the market is fully operational. If you remain in a hurry to buy and sell then you won't get anything. Understand to time the market the correct way. As rookies, you might end up doing the wrong thing at the very first go but it will prove to be a very good learning curve that will educate you on the importance of doing the right things.

The best time of exiting your position is within the first ten minutes as this is the time when the buying interest is highest. It is best advised to take advantage of this time as many companies releases Press Releases during late hours when most investors are not available and the following day they create a commotion on the first few minutes on the socks.

 Most penny stocks rushes happen between two to five days so try to exit your position within this time. The faster you secure your profits the better. Do not be caught holding the bag. Hit and run is the best strategy to make sure you stay on top in this trade.

These are the main aspects that you must consider for your penny stock trading and are sufficient for you to start your trading at the earliest. However, you must conduct further research on the topic if you wish to make the most of your penny stock trading.

When it comes to the stock market, there are many types of traders that partake in the activity of buying and selling stocks. It is important that you understand all the techniques and then decide on the one that you will choose for yourself.

Contrarian trading

Contrarian trading is the first concept that we will look at. This concept has existed for quite some time now and was popularized by Warren Buffet. The concept is extremely unique and will amuse you.

As the word suggests, a contrarian will do the contrary of what he or she should be doing. So, they will not follow the crowd and go the opposite way. They will not stock to the normal rules that most investors follow and have their own rules.

So if the market is bad and crashing, the majority will panic and start selling their stocks. But a contrarian will only start buying it. So that means the contrarian is not bothered about the fall in prices and is definitely not panicking. He is taking advantage of the opportunity and buying more of the stocks to accumulate it.

On the other hand, when the prices of the stocks are rising rapidly, the general stock trading public will decide to buy the stocks. But the contrarian will be keen on getting rid of all the stocks in his possession. So, the contrarian will always go against the general opinion of the crowd and do their own thing.

Pros of contrarian trading

The main pro of this type of investing is that, it provides the investor with an opportunity to capitalize on the market's volatility and benefit from it. The contrarian will have the chance to buy the stocks at a low price and the sell it at a good price, even if it is not the best price, it will still be a good deal. As you know, being greedy is not the right way to go about in the stock market and you must settle for whatever best you get.

The second pro of this situation is that, you have the chance to balance out the market. So when everybody is panicking and selling, you are buying it and balancing it out. If there are only sellers and no buyers then that will spell trouble. So, you can put an end to the pandemonium by becoming a contrarian and doing right by the market.

Cons of contrarian trading

As you know, contrarian trading comes with its own set of cons as well. These cons are what make the concept real.

The first con is that, the crowds might be giving up on a stock because of some formation that has leaked. Maybe the company is bad and not doing well, that might cause its stocks to lose value. During such times, you must be careful and analyze the stocks carefully before deciding to buy it.

Another disadvantage of this type of investment is that, you might have to hold on to a stock for some time before it goes up. You must know exactly when to dispose off a stock for your advantage.

As you can see, there are both pros and cons for this type of trading and it is up to you to choose or leave it.

Fundamentals trading

The next type of trading is known as fundamentals trading. As you know, when a company decides to go public with its shares, it will have to declare all of its financial details. It is this details that will help people choose the right stocks for themselves. It is possible for you to check the details of a company's financials at any point in time. All you have to do is go online and check for the details there. So the basic idea behind using the fundamental analysis is to understand the overall health of the company. You are performing the analysis to understand how the company is faring.

When you decide to check a company's financial statements, here is what you will have to look for in it.

The balance sheet

The balance sheet of a company as you know, will tell you all the debts that the company has and also mentions its assets. It is always best to choose a company that has several assets and only a few debts. A debt free company is always the best choice but it will be very difficult to find a company like that.

Income statement

The next thing to check is the company's income statement. The income statement consists of the operating and non-operating items section. The operating items section is directly related to the business that the company undertakes. It mentions clearly the expenses and incomes accrued after producing and selling the company's main products. The non-operating incomes on the other hand are those that are not directly associated with the company's products. So say for example the company decided to sell some of its assets and earned an income that will make for its non-operating income. You have to check for both when you observe the income statement of a company.

Cash flow statement

The next documents to look at are known as the cash flow statement. The cash flow statement tells you how much money is coming in and going out from the business. So you will have a clear picture of how much money is actually being circulated in the business. The cash flow statement is to be analyzed carefully to ensure that the company is able to attain consistent incomes. You have to look at the liquid assets and judge for yourself whether the company is a good place to invest in.

Apart from this, here are things that you must check in the company's balance sheet.

The earnings growth ratio is of great importance. Look for a particular pattern to see if you can easily predict how the stock's value will rise in the future.

Look at the price to earnings ratio next. The price to earnings ratio is important to calculate and you must calculate it based on the current price of the share and then divide it by the total earnings that the earnings per share. If a stock is valued at $100 and the earnings per share is $3, then the PE ratio is 33%. Here, the stock is said to be very good as the PE ratio is on the higher side. So if the PE ratio remains high then it means the stock is really good.

Next, look at the dividends that the company has been paying. Dividends play a big role when it comes to deciding whether or not a company is worth investing in. If they have been paying a consistent rate of dividend, then they are a great company to invest in.

Finally, to complete your fundamental analysis, you must check whether the company is being managed well enough. The board members run most companies and you must check whether they are operating peacefully, or there are internal problems. Stay away from the companies that have their members all fighting with each other.

Pros of fundamental trading

As you know, just like contrarian trading, fundamental trading also has its own pros and cons.

The first pro of this technique is that, it is easy for you to know how the company is operating internally. All you have to do is login to the company's website and look at their balance sheet and income statements. It will not take you a long time to do so and once you understand how to read these, you can finish doing so in express time.

The next advantage of this technique is that, you will know which stock will actually move slowly. As you know, those interested in long-term investments will decide to invest in a fundamentally sound company. So you can stay away from it and not trade in their penny stocks if you wish to find fast moving stocks. So this is a reverse pro and will help you save from investing in a slow moving stock.

Cons of fundamental trading

Fundamental trading is a good choice no doubt, but as was mentioned before, you must consider it only if you are interested in holding on to the stocks for a long time. Don't get into it if you wish to hold the stocks only for a short duration. However, don't write it off completely and ensure that you choose stocks that are fundamentally sound.

The next con is that, it will be slightly time consuming for you to go through all the individual details mentioned in the financial statements. Even if you are adept at it, it might take you around half a day or more to go through all the details of the company.

Also, your fundamental analysis will not consider the herd mentality. So you cannot be a contrarian and a fundamentalist at the same time. You won't know whether people are actually buying these stocks or you will end up being one of the few that have invested in the company.

Technical trading

The next type of analysis is known as technical trading. This is very different from fundamental trading. Here, you are not concerned about what is going on internally and are only bothered to look at the trend that the company's stock has been following.

This trend refers to whether the stock has been rising or falling. So you are basically studying the pattern that the stock is adopting. This you can do by looking at whether the stock's price has remained consistent or there have been sharp differences.

Then you will place it on a graph and check for a pattern. The pattern will tell you where the stock is headed next and whether it will rise up or fall down. You must understand whether or not the stock is predictable and you will be able to tell for sure if it is a good investment or a bad one.

Apart from you yourself checking the pattern, you must also make use of a computer to chart out an algorithm. That will provide you with further details about the stock's price volatility.

The basic idea is to understand the demand and supply of the stock. As you know, the higher the demand, the higher the price of the stock and the lower the demand, the lower the price of the stock, so you must check whether the price of the overall demand for the stock is high or low.

When you look for the movement in the volumes, make sure that you know how to interpret it correctly. You will be able to get a comprehensive graph that showcases the price trends clearly. Study this graph and understand everything that there is to about the price fluctuations and whether or not the company is a good investment choice for you.

It is understandable that you will find it a little difficult in the beginning to understand the technical of a company at the very begging, but with time and through regular practice, you will know exactly how a company's stock operates.

There are also certain online softwares that you can make use of and understand the technical of a company. In fact, it will allow you to compare two or more technical and give you a comprehensive analysis for you to pick between the two stocks.

Pros of technical trading

The very first pro of this technique is that, it helps you establish a proper trend that the stock will follow. The basic assumption of this technique is that, the stock will follow on a pre-established trend. It will rise up and fall down the same way as it has in the past. So say for example an apple stock rises mid month and falls at the end of the month. You have to know to buy it during the month end and then sell it mid month. Similarly, you have to establish the pattern for all your stocks and predict its rise and fall.

The next advantage of this technique is that, you don't have to spend too much time going through the details of the company. Unlike the fundamentals technique, you only have to establish a pattern that the stock will follow and then predict its highs and lows. Remember that you have to understand how to interpret the graph correctly and tell for sure how the stock price will move.

Cons of technical trading

Just like the pros, there are also certain cons that this technique brings with it.

The first con of this technique is that, it relies heavily on the trends alone and does not consider the company's fundamental state. So chances are, you will end up investing in a poorly managed company that is doing bad internally. That will cause you to hold on to a stock that is pretty much useless after news of it breaks.

The second con of this technique is that, the graphs will not always put out the correct trends. It will be impossible for you to predict the mentality of millions of investors and so, you will not know whether or not the stock will follow the pre determined trend. So relying heavily on trends is the wrong choice to make.

These form the different techniques that you can use to trade in the market. You must understand the pros and cons of each and only then can you choose the right one.

A.Welch

How Penny Stocks Prices Vary

As we saw in the previous chapter, there are stocks that are priced really low and traded on a regular basis in the stock market. These stocks are mostly influenced by several internal and external factors that cause its value to rise up and drop down on a daily basis. Penny stocks are slightly more predictable as their market is much different from regular stock markets. So it is easier for you to trade in penny stocks as compared to normal stocks. However, it is important to understand the various factors that influence penny stocks and how their prices vary.

The prices of penny stocks are usually influenced by their demand and supply as well as the specific assets or earnings of the particular company. This means that where there is a high demand and the supply is low, the prices will increase. This is usually the best time to sell the stocks and earn your huge margins. Since we rely on demand and supply to make profits from trading in penny stocks, you may not necessary evaluate the market but rather what could increase or decrease the prices so that you can know the best time to buy and the best time to sell.

Similarly, have an eye out on the news, as there will be stories available about the particular company. These stories will tell you whether or not the stock of a company will do well. Generally, any changes in the company's board members or an announcement of their profits will cause the price of the share to surge. Similarly, if there is a loss reported, then the price will plummet. You have to understand this trend and establish a pattern where you first check the news and then decide on a stock to buy, or stay away from. Let us look at it in detail.

The Fourth Estate and Penny Stocks

Typically, the media plays a key role in providing a catalyst in the price shift of penny stocks. Negative news of a certain company may cause their stocks to go down while positive news may make them go up. This is not always the case so a closer look and analysis is required before making your prediction. The trick is to determine whether the news is good enough to increase the price of instructions.

You can subscribe to a news journal that sends you alerts every now and then. Reading regularly is extremely important. There is no point in reading today and forgetting about it tomorrow. You must pay keen attention to the companies that issue penny stocks. Ensure that you know how to interpret the news. There can be several interpretations of the same news and you must understand it correctly, otherwise, you won't make the right choice for yourself. You must also personally go through the company's balance sheet if you want to understand it from the different points of view.

You can also watch the news and look at all the updates. They will provide you with all the best picks and help you understand which stock is a better choice for you.

Below are some sections of news to look out for as a beginner or potential investor in penny stocks to help you out

Insider Buying

If employees of a given company begin to buy shares of their own company, it is a sign that something good is coming up and so it is good to invest in shares of that company.

Reverse Mergers

This is just money in the bank. Some companies in the penny stock market are there to serve no major purpose except to function as a way for private companies to go public. This results in transfer of ownership from private individuals to the public. The private company normally has assets generates revenue but with a reverse merger, a former non-functional company suddenly acquires new assets and revenues. This is reflected by the price of stocks.

Survival from Bankruptcy

When a company announces it could be going bankrupt, their stock prices go down suddenly. Later, the company might announce that it has made a detailed plan of escaping bankruptcy and this might cause the prices of its sock to go up. This is a good chance for an investor to buy the stocks when the prices are at an all-time low and then gain in value when they go up again. Some companies though can use this technique to influence the prices of their stocks.

New Patent

A right to a new patent by a penny stock company is good news in that, it shows that in future there will be high revenue numbers.

Affiliation with A Big Company

Many people will want to be associated with big shots. If a re-known company is planning to do business with a penny stock company, then that is a clear indication of the future potential growth of that company. Big companies choose their business partners carefully. That means it is advisable to invest in that company.

Quarterly Financial Numbers

Great quarterly numbers bring about a sudden increase of prices to reflect the current quarterly numbers of the company. This can be due to various causes such as an increase in the number of contracts, royalty fees, and higher demand for products or services.

Positive Signs to Look for

As you know, prediction is everything when it comes to penny stock buying. You need to understand whether or not the price of the stock will rise soon or if it will drop down. More than the latter, it is the former that you need to consider carefully if you wish to make the most of your penny stocks.

Here are some signs that will tell you if your penny stocks are on the verge of rising up.

Money movement

The very first thing to look at is whether or not any money is moving into or out of the share. This will have a big impact on the price fluctuations of the share. If the company has introduced newer shares or split the old ones then that is also of relative significance. You can check the movement of money using the technical analysis and see whether any fresh money has been pumped into the shares. Check the on balance volume and see if it is on the upper side. If it is, then the price of the share will start to move upwards any time and you must be prepared to buy the stocks, as its share value will surge up. On the contrary, if the on balance volume is low, then the price per share will plummet. So that is indication for you to get rid of the stock as soon as possible lest you be stuck with stocks that will not fare well in the near future.

Trading volumes

The next thing to look for in a stock is the trading volume. You must look at the number of stocks being bought and sold. If there is a surge in the number of buyers then rest assured, the price of the stock will rise. You must also look at the ratio between the buyers and the sellers to have a clear idea of where the price of the stock will head. If there are many buyers and few sellers then the stock price will surely rise. But if there are lesser buyers and many sellers then the stock prices will go down. If there is a sudden movement in the volumes then you must prepare to take appropriate action. Here, there must be a double spike in the trading volumes, which will tell you whether or not it is important to note the change.

Precedence

Looking at past records is the best way to tell whether the price of a stock will rise. So look at what the company's management did in the past to understand whether your stock's price will raise or fall. The company's CEO and top management members make this decision. By checking the past records, you can see if the company has taken any action on the shares and its values. Many companies will decide to split the share and announce bonus shares, this will cause people to buy more, as the company's shares will half and turn affordable. It will subsequently cause a spike in the share's price. This is a great opportunity for you to capitalize upon and buy the shares and then sell it again when its prices have high.

News

Any company that manages to remain in the news for a long time is sure to benefit in the stock market. It is a lot like advertising. When you watch an advertisement, you will feel like buying the product. Similarly, you will feel like buying stocks of a company whose good news is doing the rounds. The news can be in regard to its fundamentals or its technical or something to do with its products. All of this will cause it to remain in the news and you can benefit from it. Just make sure you tune into the news and also hear about companies from your social circles. If there is good news then the price will definitely rise up in the near future and if there is bad news, then the price will fall for sure.

Market capture

When a company increases its market share, it is clear indication that its products are doing well in the market. You will definitely benefit from the company's stocks and must buy them at the earliest. It will also mean an increased pressure on the competitors and that will cause their shares to be affected as well. So you must check whether you have shares of their company and decide whether to hold or sell them before it gets affected further.

Results

As soon as a company announces results, there will surely be a change in its share price. If the results are good then obviously there will be a rise in the price and if the results are bad then there will be a drop in the price per share. You must be aware of when the results of the company will be announced and whether it is best for you to buy, hold or sell the stock.

Small vs big

You must understand that a large company's small shares are always better than a small company's large shares. So, look for a multi million companies whose shares are quite less in the market as opposed to a small company whose shares are more. Although contrarians will pick the latter, it is up to you to choose the type that will fit your investment need the best. With the former, it will be easier to predict the impact of market trends as opposed to the latter. So you will have something that is easy to foretell and not be stuck with shares that are not following any trend.

High low patterns

There is general belief in the stock market that a stock that has been dipping will continue to dip and a stock on the rise will continue to raise. However, the contrarian belief says a stock on the rise will dip and a dipping stock will rise. Both of these are valid views but you must look for the highest highs and the highest lows in a stock. If a stock ends up dipping below its 1 year low then the stock is in trouble, and not going to move upwards any time soon. Similarly, if the stock has hit a high much higher than its 1 year high then it is a great stock to invest in and it is best that you choose that stock for yourself.

How to Minimize Risk

As we have seen earlier on, trading in penny stocks can be quite risky especially since there is not much information about penny stock trading and your best shot is what is announced in the media. This means that you need to find all means possible to reduce your risks as much as possible. In order to minimize risk, you would need to know some common traps that many penny stocks investors have found themselves in.

Message Boards

These are literally stock cons that influence buyers and sellers to trade in the stocks while pretending to assist you with a piece of advice only to realize you have been cheated. They include pumpers and bashers. Pumpers will dupe you to buy stocks by posting "evidence" to drive prices up. When they realize that they have convinced enough people to buy stocks creating a false demand, they sell their shares and leave you stranded with your shares. Bashers on the other hand will convince you to sell the stock you bought by trying to make you think the stock is not good but in real, they are duping you. It is important to be sharp as most of these trades are a mind game. These message boards will be available in most websites that speak about stocks and those that give you details on a daily basis. There will be two or three people who will ask you to invest in a certain stock and will give you some favorable details. You might actually experience a little success initially but your luck will run out in no time and you will have to start from scratch. So you must stay as away from it as possible and ensure that you only trust reliable sources for your stock picks.

Stock Promoting E-Mails and Faxes

Some self-proclaimed gurus may send you emails or a fax to inform you that the stock prices will rise or fall. I would advice that you don't act on such information but rather do your research to make a decision. These will look like they have come from reliable places but upon investigation, you will realize that they are actually dupes that are using fake identities to get people to invest in a penny stock and increase its stock price. You should know better than that to not indulge in believing such emails and faxes, as it will only spell trouble for you.

Group Runs

These are very tricky in that they consist of an organized group of traders who come together and start buying a low volume stock. This in turn attracts attention and people turn try to buy them. When prices shoot up because of the demand, these groups sell their shares at high prices and leave the last person to buy at the highest price demand of the day counting his or her loss when the demand suddenly shifts back to its low. An advice here is that you can invest in this stock but you need to be fast; make hay while the sun shines by selling when the prices are still high. You must know clearly whether you are a day trader or will hold on to the stocks for long. If you are the former then get rid of your stocks the same day and if you are the latter, then hold on to it for at least 2 days.

Average News

Nobody wants to be average. Average news does not make a kill in the penny stock market. They always lead to average returns. Therefore, for you to be influenced by some news to invest in some penny stock, make sure the news are good enough to make a hit. Don't settle for it even if it is a great company. Your money is of value to you and you must tread carefully in the stock market.

Too Much News

Companies that give too many press releases that are intended to influence the prices of penny stocks should be approached with a lot of caution. As a beginner, you should do research on recent press releases of that company and see whether they are just trying to make value of their stocks in order to influence prices to go up. Experienced traders will not invest in such companies and so should you.

S-8 Filing

This is when a company files a document to the Stock Exchange Commission telling them that they have increased the number of shares in stock. The key factor is to check on demand and supply. Now that the supply is high, it is prudent to stay away from such investments.

Unavoidable Rules of Day Trading Penny Stocks

As you begin your journey in penny stocks trading, you would need to be aware of some important rules of trading in penny stocks.

These are rules that you must swear by if you wish to make the most of your penny stock trading. These have been formulated keeping in mind the different ways in which the market operates and what you must consider when you pick a penny stock to trade with.

Always stick to your guts

It is important when trading in penny stocks to set your own rules and regulations and make sure you stick to them. Don't be easily swayed unless you are sure of your judgment. Many times, it is easy to get carried away and buy stocks that you do not actually want for yourself. You will only buy them owing to a suggestion that you get from somewhere. Doing so will cause you to repent your decision later. You must stock to your plan and gut feeling.

You must know what you are doing and whether that is the right choice for you. If your gut is telling you to not buy a stock then don't know matter what you hear from another person. But if your gut asks you to buy a stock even if it has a bad review then buy it. In addition, once you have set up your maximum percentage gain and maximum percentage loss, stick to this and don't be in a rush to spend money; take your time.

Only use money that you are ready to put to risk

Trading in penny stocks can be viewed as a gamble from one viewpoint. Always do play with money you are not afraid to lose. It is advisable that you do not use funds that you are emotionally attached to like money for paying your bills or for doing other important things. This is because you are likely to make a better-informed decision. If you know that the money you want to invest is meant for paying bills and if you are unable to pay bills, you may be in trouble, you are likely to be too conservative and go all out in making an investment. This however does not mean that now you use money you are not afraid to lose that you can make uninformed decisions. At the beginning of the month, set aside some money that you will only use for your trading. This money will be used sparingly and you are prepared to take a risk on it. Remember that there are no guarantees in the stock market and you might actually end up losing money there. You will have to look into the consequences of your investments just as you would look at the positives. A sound investor will ensure that he has calculated the risk before putting the money into the stock market. So you must do the same if you wish to gain from your investments.

Educate yourself about the market everyday

It is important to study the market on a daily basis to keep abreast with the underlying factors causing the changes in the prices of stocks. Ask yourself whether you should have traded in certain stocks or not after the market has closed down to make you prepare well for your next trade in penny stocks. If you think you can read a book or two and understand everything that there is to about penny stocks then you are wrong. Even old hands who have been trading in stocks for several years will be open to learning from the market on a daily basis. The markets will not always be the same and you must understand the differences in the situations and take with you a new experience. It is ideal that you take note of everything and ensure that you have it with you for easy reference in the future.

Learn from your experience.

For you to make it in the penny stock trading, you must learn to accept your mistakes, learn from them and move on to become better in penny stocks trading. The more you learn from your past and use it in your current dealings the better, as you will be able to come out successful in the penny stock market. Don't keep thinking about it and worrying though. The stock market can be extremely punishing at times but it will also pay back if you know how to play it right. So don't be over enthusiastic about a loss and end up making the same mistake again in a bid to correct the previous one. A wise investor will know a situation and its impact before it arrives. That is only possible if you understand the different situations and learn from your prior experiences.

Be realistic

When determining your profit percentage gain, always try to be realistic. Setting a too high percentage profit gain means a high risk of making a loss. So be realistic and set it at a point of maximum possible gain but don't set it too low either, as that will mean little or no gain. It is recommended to set the profit percentage gain at around 10% for daily trading and setting it at 20% for trends simply because trends are more determinable and you can be sure of something good. Many might see 10% as too low but putting in mind 10 % for a whole month added together can make some good earnings. So do not aim too high; it is always good to play safe. If the opportunity presents itself for you to take an exit on a stock then grab the opportunity immediately. Don't think you will be able to go higher and gain more on it in the near future. What if the pattern reverses and the price of the stock starts to fall. You will be in trouble for it.

Be a quick decision maker

When it comes to making a decision, you need to be fast. There is no time or chance to waste. However, that does not mean you dive in into any bid without giving it a second thought. Do not just think but also think fast. If you keep hesitating, you will end up buying when the trade is at its highest and you will end up being caught pants down. You will be the last man standing at a loss as the demand usually reduces suddenly. Do not chase a stock up too long. This is especially dangerous during the wee hours of trade. You will not know whether to sell a stock or buy it. You will end up losing money and wonder why you did such a thing. Strike while the rod is hot but remember not to get too close to the highest point of the wave. As I said, you might be caught off guard.

Keep your funds liquid everyday

When you buy a stock, make sure you sell it on that same day or some few days later to ensure that you have liquid assets. This is important simply because you need the money to trade with especially when a good deal comes up. If you do not do that, you will be missing an opportunity that might show up on the next day only to find your hands tied. One more thing to note is that most of the penny stocks show a huge growth in a single day and then it dies down the following day. So grab the opportunity while you have it. Buy and sell the penny stocks the same day, as you cannot be sure of tomorrow.

Be your own boss in making decisions

A wise man makes his own decisions. If you have to listen to any advice, let it not be from a person trying to convince you to buy or sell this stock, as you will be duped. People have their own interests at heart so have your own close to you. Make independent decisions, as this is the rule if you want to be successful in penny stocks trading. If you are easily swayed, then it is good to remember that in penny stocks, prices also keep shifting. If you have a broker who tells you to buy and sell stocks, you must know to say yes or no. They are only meant to help you pick good stocks, it is up to you to research it and tell them whether or not you are interested in it. The same applies to websites that suggest the stocks to you. They are suggesting it based on their analysis of the stock. If you think it is not a good investment then you have all the right to refuse it.

Only go for big news and nothing less

Earlier on, I stated that some news could be used just to influence the trade while in real sense the news does not carry much weight only that they have been made to look like something big is coming. Average news will give you average returns. Only big news can make a kill so be on the lookout for something big when it comes to news.

In order to avoid making huge mistakes in trading in penny stocks, it is advisable that you are aware of some common mistakes that people make. Below is a list of common mistakes people do when trading in penny stocks:

*Pursuing an entry point above 50%

This is a very common mistake happens within the minutes or after the opening bell. Never assume that the prices will go up. The current rapid upward movement usually is short lived. Before you know it, you will find that the prices have gone down to low again. Avoid a stock that gains within short periods and concentrate on those that take long to gain.

*Trade of between 25% to 50% of your total balance on any given trade to reduce the overall trader account balance limits.

*Social media and message board hype.

*Holding your position for too long because we aim at catching a 25 to 50% gain in a given trade. Therefore, once you reach your target it is prudent to exit your position.

*Buying randomly is not good as this can be because of message boards, a tip from a forum, neighbor or friend, which can be misleading.

Tips and Tricks For Successful Penny Stocks Trading

Penny stocks trading can promise huge returns when done right. We will look at some useful tips that can be of great help in helping you increase your yields.

Don't hire penny stockbrokers unless you really have to

One of the most important things to do is not to hire penny stockbrokers unless you really have to. These brokers usually require higher commissions and multiple fees, which may eat into your penny stock earnings. Furthermore, penny stockbrokers will be paid a commission whether you experience financial gains or losses. So they will not put in the efforts to ensure that you always remain in gains. There are also theories that the company will try to employ those that have good convincing skills and even when you are not interested in a particular stock, you will end up buying it. Look for a discount online trading place that will give you the opportunity to trade penny stocks independently and not depend on the brokers to do your buying and selling.

Don't invest in penny stocks whose trading volume is less than 100000 per day

You should also choose the penny stocks you want to invest in very carefully. Try as much as possible to avoid those that trade in volume less than 100,000 per day, as they are likely to be less liquid. As you know, the price per share of these stocks is very low so you must look for those that are actually being traded and not merely having a good low price. If the prices of such stocks start coming down, you are unlikely to find someone willing to buy since the shares' volume is quite low.

Do not invest in penny stocks from the same industry

The trick to making it big in whatever kind of investment you are making is to diversify. This is the same case with investing in penny stocks. Never invest in penny stocks in the same field of industry; however good the industry may be doing since if such an industry starts crushing, you would lose all your investments. It is always best to diversify your risk when you invest in the stock market. If you think the IT industry is faring well and it will pay you well to buy stocks from companies that belong to that industry then it is best to reconsider your evaluation and split your risk to ensure your investment's safety.

Focus your attention on company behind the stock

While focusing your attention on the actual stock is a good strategy, focusing your attention on the company behind the stock is the best strategy. You should know if the company is working on any technologies, new products or services and innovative products, as this will affect the price of their stocks. This best way to do so is by looking at their fundamentals and also reading their news. These are the best places for you to study the company's internal details. If you have knowledge about the company's products then do a self-analysis to understand where the company is headed.

Always be informed

You should also ensure that you are informed of everything that may be happening in the penny stock market. Ensure that each day you scan through publications or other resource that may have some coverage on penny stock activities.

A.Welch

How To Successfully Trade Penny Stocks

Knowing what you do now, which is the important basics of penny stock trading, here are several ways to trade in penny stocks that can help you increase your chances of successfully trading them and reducing (not eliminating) the associated risks.

Don't focus on the success stories

In his best-selling book The Art Of Thinking Clearly, Rolf Dobelli wrote about a psychological habit called The Survivorship Bias, which is one of the obstacles to thinking clearly, which you'll need if you want to succeed in penny stocks trading. According to Dobelli, the survivorship bias is our tendency to overestimate our chances of succeeding in our chosen endeavors because of our – and possibly society's – tendency to focus more on the possibility of success than the risks of failing. This is exacerbated by most people's tendency to label people who are either cautious or realistic as either party-poopers, pessimists or worse, failure-minded people. It's as if being mindful of possible risks and dangers is a mortal sin that can't be forgiven in this life or the next!

But as Dobelli points out, it is a bias because it tends to glorify positivity over realism. In fact, much of your success – be it in penny stocks trading or in life – can be learned through the stories and lessons of failures. Consider Thomas Edison's success in inventing the light bulb, which clearly changed the human race for the better! He learned more from the failed experiments than from the one single successful one. He said that he didn't "fail" in those numerous experiments that didn't work out because with each failed experiment, he learned another way not to create or assemble the light bulb. By knowing the many, many things that don't work, he was able to avoid them and narrow down the ideas that worked.

Funny but in my personal trading experience, be it with penny stocks or exchange-traded ones, the most unforgettable lessons were from my or my friends' trading failures. It's probably because the more powerful motivation in my doing many things in life is avoidance of pain, the other motivation being love of pleasure.

When you focus on the success stories, you can greatly overestimate your chances of success and blind you so much to clear signals, which may cause you to lose money in your trading. It's not that you should disregard success stories. No, that's not the point. The point is to have a balanced view or approach – consider both the successes and failures. In fact, for every success story or principle you find, look for 2 or 3 stories of failure and loss. In as much as you'll need to know what to do to earn great returns from your penny stocks trading, you should also learn what not to do in order to keep your shirt on and succeed more often.

Focus on the disclaimers instead of tips

More often than not, penny stocks are sold not bought. What this means is in many cases, the demand for such is weak and for investors to snap them up, they need to be actively promoted and sold, compared to exchange-listed shares of stock of established companies like Apple, Inc. Most penny stocks are sold via free emails and newsletters that give "tips" about the penny stocks being sold. The problem with these newsletters and emails, however, is transparency. Penny stocks trading expert Timothy Sykes says that these newsletters and emails don't give tips out of a heart of sincere goodness and desire for you to succeed. If you check out the bottom-most part of these emails and newsletters, you'll find their disclaimers about the email and the tips therein. You'll realize, if you check out these disclaimers, that the people or institutions that emailed you those free tips about penny stocks of particular companies are actually paid by the companies that issued those penny stocks in the email or newsletters to pitch their stocks and provide good public exposure for such. Although exposure isn't necessarily an evil thing, Sykes says that almost every penny stocks newsletter or email pitch promises that aren't entirely true in order to promote the penny stocks in question.

There's a huge difference when a stock reaches an all-time high in terms of trading price due to record earnings and when it does so simply because intensive promotion of said stock by a couple of email and newsletter senders. How do you know which is which? One of the best ways is to pay attention to a very important part of such emails and newsletters that are often times taken for granted: the disclaimer. If a newsletter or email giving tips on particular penny stocks don't have a disclaimer, disregard it because off the bat, you already know it isn't legit. It's because the SEC requires senders of such emails and newsletters to put disclaimers on their emails and newsletters and it is through these disclaimers that you'll be able to see potential conflicts of interest. Without a disclaimer, it's clear that there already exists a conflict of interest and it's normally between yours and theirs.

Lastly, Sykes says that these newsletters are often paid merely to increase demand for a stock by pump up it up and rarely do these give you tips on when to sell. If ever they do, according to him, it would've been too late. Think of it this way – if a penny stock were really a good one, there'd be very little need to promote them via newsletters and email. Investors would flock to it and you, as an active investor, would most certainly hear or read about it one way or another.

Sell fast

Remember that you're trading penny stocks, which is different from long-term investing. Long-term investing involves a buy-and-hold approach and is long term in nature, which requires you don't sell or liquidate your position quickly. Trading, on the other hand, is like speed dating – it's all about speed! And one of the cardinal rules for success of such is being able to quickly liquidate as soon as you reach your realistically set profit target. As with some romantic relationships, being clingy when it comes to penny stocks trading can spell disaster for you. Consider my trading experience many, many years ago.

After doing a good enough research, I bought stocks of one of the up-and-coming but relatively popular real estate companies. Within 2 days, the price of the stock went up by about 5%. In the next 3 days, it went up further by another 5%. During the 1st trading week since I bought the stock, I already earned 10% net profit. Trading sense would dictate that I already liquidate. I mean, if a 10% annual return is already in and by itself a huge gain, what more a 10% return in a week!

Being the relatively inexperienced – and stubborn one if I may add – trader that I was at that time, I held on to the position and refused to liquidate. I made all possible excuses for doing so such as technical analysis charts that I felt indicated a continuation in the rise of its price, among others. Fortunately, the stock's price did rise further. In about 2 weeks since I bought the stocks, I already made 30% in paper profits. You would've thought that given my rather fortunate experience, I would've liquidated already, right? Wrong! I became even clingier.

On the 3rd week, the stock's price dipped and the return on my investment was down to a respectable 20%, which was still quite remarkable for a mere 3-week-old investment. You would've thought I'd liquidate by then and cash in on my profits, right? Wrong! I still let my clinginess rule my otherwise objective trading strategy and insisted that the dip was a mere "correction" and that the bullish or upward trend will eventually continue and persist.

It never did. To cut the long story short, I held on to the stock until I suffered losses on my position. Had I liquidated early considering my strategy was one of trading, I could've earned a handsome 10% return on the first week or even 30% in a mere 2 weeks. But because I was quick to buy and slow to sell, I suffered the consequences.

Remember that when it comes to penny stocks trading, greed is your worst enemy.

Don't rely on what management says

In the world of marketing, testimonies about a product or service are very important. It's because to some extent, it gives you a glimpse of how good – or bad – the marketed product or service really is. Customers who give reviews of a particular product or service are deemed to be good sources of information on the purported benefits or superiority of a product because of the perceived lack of bias as people who don't stand to benefit from increase sales of the product or service. When businesses are revealed to have paid or have given other fringe benefits to people in exchange for or to encourage good public testimonies, the public backlash is often wicked and unrelenting. Testimonies or promotions need to be as free from perceived ulterior motives as possible. They need to be perceived as independent from any undue influence.

Management's statements and press releases about their respective companies, whether we like it or not, should be taken with a grain of salt. In fact, it may be better to disregard them altogether. Why? It's because they have a vested interest in making such statements. There's a 50-50 chance that they're not entirely truthful because they are under shareholders' pressure to drive up their companies' stock prices in order to, among other things, raise funds to continue operating the business profitably. With the relatively scarcer information about penny stock companies compared to exchange listed ones, it's quite a challenge to validate the veracity of penny stock companies' management's claims as to corporate health and performance.

Given that the management of penny stock companies are innocent until proven otherwise, you shouldn't put all your faith in their statements but merely consider them together with other important information such as audited financial statements (where available) and industry performance and outlook. You should also check out "rumor mills" like online forums and group discussions to get a feel of what other people know about a particular penny stock you're considering trading in the immediate future.

Totally dismissing or disregarding managements' statements about their respective penny stock companies is a rather extreme measure much like throwing away the baby together with the bath water. Relying on them is like throwing away the baby and keeping the bath water. Throw away the bath water but keep the baby by considering managements' statements in conjunction with other seemingly more objective sources of information to increase your chances of penny stock trading success and lower your risks of failing in doing so.

Never short sell

If you're not familiar with the term, this is what it means: Short selling is a speculative activity where you sell something that you don't have with the expectation that by the time you need to deliver the goods, the price of such goods would've dropped significantly in order for you to make a good profit. Short selling is normally done by borrowing shares you don't own, selling those shares and when the price goes down, you buy the same number of shares to return to the person or institution you borrowed the shares from. Short selling is a popular strategy among traders in bear markets, i.e., when the prices of securities like stocks are on a downtrend. The idea is to sell today at a higher price and buy the security to be delivered later at a lower price. It's just a variant of the trading success formula of buying low and selling high where you sell first before buying.

Short selling has got to be one of the most ingenious trading strategies ever conceived by the trading man. It has to be since it allows you to make a killing even when the market for a particular security is on the decline. Despite the seemingly bulletproof logic behind the strategy, it carries with it a great risk of you losing your money and your reputation. Considering that penny stock trading in and by itself is already a higher-risk proposition compared to investing in exchange-listed stocks with huge market capitalizations with already established names.

Short selling penny stocks can significantly increase your risk for potentially huge losses. One reason is compared to publicly listed stock on organized exchanges, penny stocks quoted on the OTC Board aren't mandated by law to be registered with the SEC nor are they required to submit current financial statements. As such, prices of penny stocks tend to be volatile and open to manipulation, both of which can significantly affect share prices very abruptly. When volatility or manipulation suddenly drives up the prices of the penny stocks you shorted, you are in an enviable position of suffering potentially huge losses.

There are many times when you wonder if it is a good idea to short sell a stock that is actually doing badly or is on the decline. But remember that you are only adding to the chaos and worsening the situation. Don't lose your cool in a bad situation and remain put.

Another reason why short selling penny stocks can work more to your disadvantage is the problem of liquidity or availability of such shares in the future when you need to buy them back. Often times, penny stocks are very thinly traded compared to their exchange-listed counterparts and when you need to cover a very short position, volume may not be enough to allow you to do so leaving you with a tarnished image, losses or both.

Penny stock trading is already risky as it is so my advice: leave short selling to the experts who have a wealth of experience on the practice as well as deep pockets.

Focus on high trading volume

Remember about liquidity being a key issue of trading in penny stocks? The key indicator for liquidity is trading volume. Why? The bigger the volume, the greater the interest in the penny stock is, which indicates a very good potential for price increase and a much better chance of getting out of your position quickly. If you choose to trade a thinly traded penny stock, i.e., one that has low trading volume, the risk of its price going down is high as well as your liquidity risk, i.e., the ability to liquidate your shares on time and at the price you want.

You may ask: What makes for a high daily trading volume? For purposes of this strategy, consider penny stocks with an average daily trading volume of at least 100,000 shares to be one with high trading volume. Anything less, stay away from them.

To show you the importance of trading volume in reducing your risks, consider this example with 2 scenarios. You bought 100,000 shares of Penny Stock A (PSA for brevity) at $0.20 per share for a total cost of $20,000. In scenario A, PSA's stock price went up to $0.25 per share for a paper profit of $0.05 per share or $5,000 equal to a return-on-investment of 25%, which is quite a lot. If PSA's daily average trading volume is just, say, 50,000 shares, you won't be able to unload all your shares at $0.25 per share. You'll have to sell the remaining 50,000 shares the next day but there's a chance the price will have changed by then. Good if it goes up, but if it goes down to, say $0.23 per share, your trading profit for the 50,000 remaining shares will just be $0.03 per share or $1,500 and if you add it to the ones you already sold earlier, your total profit goes down to only $4,000 from $5,000 initially. That's a difference of $1,000 or 20%!

In scenario B, PSA's stock price goes down to $0.19 the day after and you decide to liquidate. If the stock's average daily trading volume is high, proceeds of the sale of all 100,000 shares of PSA will yield you $19,000 or a loss of $1,000 on your $20,000 investment – a 5% loss on investment. If average daily trading volume however, is at only 50,000 shares, you'll have to share the other half of your holdings the day after. If assuming for the sake of argument that the share price of PSA falls further to $0.18 per share, your proceeds for the remaining half of the shares will only be $9,000. Adding up the proceeds of the 50,000 shares sold at $0.19 per share – total of $9,500 – and the second 50,000 at $0.18 per share, total proceeds will be $18,500, which is $500 less than if you were able to sell all the day before. That translates to an additional 3% loss on your $20,000 investment that brings your loss on investment from only 5% to 8%.

Create and strictly implement trading stops

What are trading stops? These are price levels you determine to be action triggers to either buy or sell shares of stocks. Often, they're called stop-loss limits or take-profit triggers, the former being the price at which you'll have to liquidate your position in order to limit your losses and the latter being the price at which you need to liquidate to realize a minimum amount of profit.

Why create or set up trading stops? It's to help prevent you from trading with your heart instead of your head, like what happened to me in the example I gave in the section on selling fast. Emotions have the uncanny ability to muddle one's good judgment, especially when it comes to trading stocks. I can lay the claim to being an expert on that matter because I have experienced losses on account of trading by heart and not by logic.

So what is the ideal trading stop levels for you when it comes to penny stocks trading? The key lies in your risk tolerance or capacity for potential losses. Ask yourself how much losses can you tolerate both in terms of percentage and $ value? If for example, you determine your loss limit at 5%, your take profit levels at 10%, and that you're willing to start trading with $1,000, you can compute for stop-loss and profit-taking trading stops as follows if you bought 1,250 shares of Penny Stock B (PSB) at $0.80 per share:

Loss Trading Stop = Purchase Price X (1 - %limit)

Loss Trading Stop = $0.80 x (1 − 5%)

Loss Trading Stop = $0.80 x (95%)

Loss Trading Stop = $0.76 per share

Take Profit Trading Stop = Purchase Price X (1 + %limit)

Take Profit Trading Stop = $0.80 X (1 + 5%)

Take Profit Trading Stop = $0.80 X (105%)

Take Profit Trading Stop = $0.88

There you have it – your trading stops of $0.76 and $0.88. When your stock price hits either price stops, it's time to liquidate.

The easy part of this trading tactic is determining your trading stops. The challenging part is implementing it, considering that you'll be going up against your emotions. Believe me, emotions are powerful so never underestimate it and give it an inch to rule your trading activities. You'll have to be strong and resist the urge to hold on to your penny stock once its price hits either trading stops. Yes, these stops aren't prophets that can perfectly predict what's gonna happen to the penny stocks' prices but they do help you minimize trading with your heart and help you rely more on objective logic in doing so, which increases your success of trading penny stocks successfully.

Never settle for less than the best

If you don't settle for anything less than the best value for your money when shopping for a coffee maker, television, car, house or even a spouse, shouldn't you be doing the same for penny stocks to trade in? Compared to the choosing inferior quality stuff, choosing the wrong penny stock is much like choosing the wrong spouse: it can be quite costly.

When we say choosing the best penny stocks for trading, we're talking about companies with great earnings or whose penny stock prices are breaking out of 52-week highs with an average daily trading volume of at least 250,000 shares. Why is this so?

First, let's consider earnings. The value of stocks, be it penny or regular, are hinged greatly on income, particularly expectations about future income. It stands to reason that penny stock companies that aren't doing well earnings-wise can't be expected to produce great income in the near or medium term. It's like betting on a power lifter attempting to bench press 500 pounds. Would you bet on a power lifter to press 500 pounds if the heaviest the dude has ever pressed is just 300? Rational expectations, baby!

Second, consider trading volume. It may not do you much good to buy 100,000 shares of a penny stock of a company with great earnings with an average daily trade of only 5,000 shares! Remember, you'll only truly realize profits from your trading when you are able to sell the shares at a higher price. No matter how high the price goes up, your profits will just be considered "paper" if you're still holding on to them. Remember liquidity and how important it is making the most profit out of your trading? The bigger the volume, the higher the liquidity and consequently, your potential profit.

Lastly, why consider if its stock price has broken through the previous 52-week high? Despite the absence of an airtight set of arguments and evidences, it is believed that the previous 52-week high price level is a good resistance level, which is defined as a price level that acts as some sort of a psychological cap for many investors. It's the price at which many investors think prices bounce off from and start to go down, much like the ceiling that limits the height at which helium-filled balloons can fly. Once prices break through or exceed a solid resistance level, it's believed that the investors' mental price barrier has been broken and that it signifies a new period in which a stock's price will continue to rise even more. It's like the ceiling caving in, which allows the balloon to fly even higher.

Limit your position size

Your penny stock trading profits and losses are a function of price movements and position size, i.e., number of shares. It stands to reason therefore that the bigger your position, the higher your potential trading income...and losses. In this regard, you should carefully consider your position's size in order to strike a good balance between profit and risk.

Consider a $0.05 price movement in the shares of penny stock C (PSC). If you bought 50,000 shares of PSC and the price moved upward, you'd earn a profit of $2,500.00 compared to only $1,250 if you just bought half the number of shares or 25,000 shares only. However, if it moved downward by the same amount, you'd suffer a larger loss of $2,500.00 compared to a loss of only $1,250.00 with a smaller position of only 25,000 shares. Given all things equal, the size of your position can spell a big difference in your penny stocks trading success or failure.

Another reason for limiting your position size is for liquidity. The smaller your position size is with respect to a particular penny stock's average daily trading volume, the easier it is to liquidate such a position and lock on your profits or minimize trading losses. The higher your position size relative to average daily trading volume, the higher your liquidity risk becomes.

So how do you determine your optimal position size for trading a particular penny stock? There are 2 ways to do it: liquidity approach and risk tolerance approach. Using the liquidity approach, you simply limit your position size in a particular penny stock to no more than a certain percentage of its average daily trading volume. If for example, penny stock D's (PSD) average daily trading volume is 100,000 shares and you set your position limit to 20% of that volume, your maximum position size in PSD is 20,000 shares.

If you choose to use the risk tolerance approach to limiting your position size, you'll need to determine the maximum loss you're willing to tolerate both in percentage terms and $ amount then use the following formula to determine position size in $ terms:

$ Maximum Position Size = Maximum Loss in $ Amount ÷ Maximum Loss in %

For example, you determined your loss tolerances at 5% and $100 per trade, your position size using the formula would be:

Maximum Position Size = $100 ÷ 5%

Maximum Position Size = $2,000

Once you determine your position size in $ terms, simply calculate the number of shares by dividing the amount over the current trading price to determine your maximum position size in terms of shares.

Love is a crime

Brian May, the former guitarist of the great rock band Queen, wrote a song about the dangers of loving someone too much, which was aptly titled Too Much Love Will Kill You. Although the context of that song was romantic love and feelings for an actual person, the same song can also be sung for penny stock trading! Loving a penny stock too much can make you clingy and refuse to let go of the stock when you need to. Too much love or attachment to a penny stock can cloud your better judgment and increase your risks for unsuccessful penny stock trading.

Attachment to a particular penny stock – also known in emo circles as being clingy – is a result of several things such as greed, focusing too much on success stories (survivorship bias) and relying primarily on management's statements and press releases, among other things. So how do you become or continue staying detached from your favorite penny stock?

First, you need to be content when you already achieve or slightly exceed your target profit. This is a good way to control or even overcome one of our biggest weaknesses: greed. Contrary to what Gordon Gekko's[1] doctrine that greed is good, it isn't. Look no further than my experience with that real estate company stock where I wasted paper profits of 30% in a couple of weeks

---

The primary character in the movie Wall Street and Wall Street: Money Never Sleeps.

because of my desire for even more profits and reluctance to cash in on what was already a very, very good return. Greed is possibly the most powerful emotion that perpetuates a strong clinginess to particular penny stocks.

Second, you need to consciously overcome or address the survivorship bias by doing your homework and researching on penny stock horror stories too instead of just honing on success stories that are often exaggerated or worse, fabricated. Learning the horror stories can help ground or level your expectations and in the process, significantly reduce your attachment to a particular penny stock.

Lastly, you should significantly lessen your dependence or reliance on management's press releases and promise concerning their penny-stock issuing company's earnings and financial health. As you learned earlier, their statements should be taken with a grain of salt and validated or considered together with other more objective sources of information and data because of conflict of interest that's inherent with their position in the penny stock issuing company and the bonuses that come with their ability to increase the company's penny stock price. As we noted in an earlier section, some of the best sources for validating management's statements and press releases include their audited financial statements, forums and discussion groups on their penny stocks or the penny stocks market and expert estimates and forecasts of the future expectations for the industry to which a particular penny stock company belongs to.

Key Take Aways

The very first take away from this book is to thoroughly understand what penny stocks are. Penny stocks are those that are valued at less than $5. These stocks are generally not traded in the stock market and are traded over the counter. You must know whether or not these stocks are good choices for you to trade in, before you decide to invest in them. Understand every little detail about these stocks before investing in them if you want to make a killing in the penny stock market.

The next thing to do here; is get started in the stock market and trade in these penny stocks. For that, you need to take care of certain things like registering with a brokering company, getting yourself a computer, an Internet connection and employing an appropriate broker. These are all essential when you wish to start trading in penny stocks. It is important that you also understand paper trading, as penny stocks will encourage you to trade in papers before you bust out your actual money. You must try and maintain a journal to record all your experiences right from the first day of trade.

Penny stocks, as compared to regular stocks, are easier to predict and there are only a few things to consider, in order to understand, which way the stocks will move. These things include buy volumes, reverse mergers, bankruptcy announcements, dividend sharing, market capture etc. All these will impact the stock's price and you must observe them to understand what way the stock price will move.

There are three main ways in which you can trade in the stock market and they include the contrarian method, the fundamental approach and the technical analysis. Each of these come with their fair share of pros and cons and you must understand each before making your choice.

The basic idea behind making money using the penny stocks is to buy them at their lowest and then sell them at their highest. For that to happen, you have to observe the stock all through the day and know when to hold it and when to sell it. It pays to wake up early and do some research before the market starts. If you know that a penny stock is going to fall and rise steeply, then you must observe it for an entire day before investing in it.

Remember that it is always best to exit when the price is high, than wait on it to go any higher. You will risk gaining a profit on it and end up settling for a loss. So leave all your greed out of your trading and settle for the best price on offer even if it is not the highest price. There are absolutely no guarantees in the stock market and it is best that you tread carefully and calculate your risk before investing in penny stocks.

There can be many people out there posing to be stock market experts, but in reality, they will be scammers. You must be wary of them and not trust their proposals. They might send you emails and faxes but you must ignore them and can also report them. Similarly, you must not take part in message board stocks that are all about mind games. You will not experience consistent profits through their stocks at the very beginning, but will start experiencing heavy losses sooner or later.

You must compulsorily make use of a stop loss mechanism when it comes to penny stocks. These are meant to help you save money and will ensure that your money will not get stuck in the wrong place for a long time. Even if you lose on some money, it is best to settle for a stop loss mechanism as you can easily make back the money from a better stock. Remember to not get emotionally attached to any stock!

Finally, remember to always do your research for any stock and invest in it only if you are confident that it will do well. Don't settle for average when you can get the best!

A.Welch

Conclusion

Thank you again for purchasing this book!

I hope this book was able to help you understand what penny stocks are and how to make it big in penny stocks. If you want to start making money from investing in penny stocks, you had better start now as all that is remaining is putting into action what you have learnt.

Finally, if you enjoyed this book, please share your thoughts and post a review on Amazon!

Thank you and good luck!

CPSIA information can be obtained
at www.ICGtesting.com
Printed in the USA
FFOW01n2132021115
18281FF